CONTENTS

03

HOW TO DO MULTITHREADING WITH JAVASCRIPT

INTRODUCTION

Node.js is capable of doing multithreading with the release of version 13 onwards.

Most JavaScript developers believe Node.js is single-threaded, which handles multiple operations by non-blocking asynchronous callback processes and doesn't support multithreading, but it is not valid anymore. On Node.js version 13, a new module called worker threads is there to implement multithreading.

Even though non-blocking asynchronous callback could handle multiple operations very efficiently, functions requiring massive CPU utilization like encryption block other processes, Node.js' performance is weak for such a scenario. The worker thread module overcomes that weakness by isolating the function, which takes high CPU usage into a separate thread and processing it in the background and won't block any other process.

IMPLEMENTATION

Typically in Node.js, the main thread handle all the operations. With the help of an example, here demonstrated how to create another thread for processing an operation. This example has two API, the first API will process the function on the main thread, and the other API will process the function on a separate thread. The below code snippet shows the basic structure of the example.

```
/*
 * File Name: index.js
 * Description: This is the main thread
 */
const express = require("express");
const app = express();
const port = 3000;
app.get("/", (req, res) => {
res.send("Process function on main thread.");
});
app.get("/seprate-thread", (req, res) => {
res.send("Process function on seprate thread.")
});
app.listen(port, () => {
console.log(`Example app listening at
http://localhost:${port}`);
});
```

As a first step, we add a function on the main thread, and as a next step, we add the same function on another thread. The function used will be getSum, which will return the cumulative sum up to the limit value given as an argument. After adding the getSum function to the main thread, the code snippet becomes like below.

```
/*
 * File Name: index.js
 * Description: This is the main thread
 */
const express = require("express");
const app = express();
const port = 3000;
const getSum = (limit) => {
let sum = 0;
for (let i = 0; i < limit; i++) {
    sum += i;
}
return sum;
};
app.get("/", (req, res) => {
const result = getSum(1000);
res.send(`Processed function getSum on main
thread and result: ${result}`);
});
app.get("/seprate-thread", (req, res) => {
res.send("Process function getSum on seprate
thread.");
});
app.listen(port, () => {
console.log(`Example app listening at
http://localhost:${port}`);
});
```

The next step is to add the same function on another thread, and it could do as follow.

- Importing the worker thread module to the main thread.

```
const { Worker } = require("worker_threads");
```

- Create another file, seprateThread.js, for defining the function getSum to run on another thread.

- Create an instance of the worker thread module and provide the pathname to the newly created file.

```
const seprateThread =
new Worker(__dirname + "/seprateThread.js");
```

- Starting a new thread

```
seprateThread.on("message", (result) =>
{res.send(`Processed function getSum on
seprate thread: ${result}`);});
```

- Sending data to the new thread.

```
seprateThread.postMessage(1000);
```

Finally, the main thread will be like the below code snippet.

```
/*
 * File Name: index.js
 * Description: This is the main thread
 */
const express = require("express");
const { Worker } = require("worker_threads");
const app = express();
const port = 3000;
const getSum = (limit) => {
let sum = 0;
for (let i = 0; i < limit; i++) {
    sum += i;
}
return sum;
};
app.get("/", (req, res) => {
const result = getSum(1000);
res.send(`Processed function getSum on main
thread and result: ${result}`);
});
app.get("/seprate-thread", (req, res) => {
const seprateThread = new Worker(__dirname
"/seprateThread.js");
```

```
seprateThread.on("message", (result) => {
res.send(`Processed function getSum on sepra
thread: ${result}`);
});
seprateThread.postMessage(1000);
});
app.listen(port, () => {
console.log(`Example app listening at
http://localhost:${port}`);
});
```

Thus a new thread is created from the main thread. Let us put the getSum function on the newly created thread, so defines that function on the file seprateThread.js. After defining, the new thread is supposed to send the result back to the main thread; check the below code for reference.

```
/*
 * File Name: seprateThread.js
 * Description: This is another thread
 */
const { parentPort } = require("worker_threads")
const getSum = (limit) => {
  let sum = 0;
  for (let i = 0; i < limit; i++) {
    sum += i;
  }
  return sum;
};
parentPort.on("message", (limit) => {
 const result = getSum(limit);
 parentPort.postMessage(result);
});
```

In the above example, you could see seprateThread.postMessage() function used by the main thread to communicate with the child thread. Likewise, parentPort.postMessage() used by the child thread to communicate with the main thread. The below figure illustrates the communication between the child and the main thread.

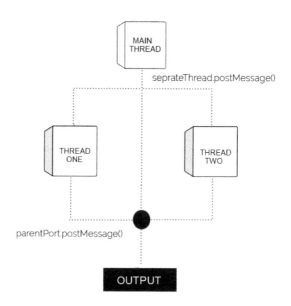

FEATURES

- Each thread has separate v8 engines.

- Child threads could communicate with each other.

- Child threads could share the same memory.

- An initial value could be passed as an option while starting the new thread.

CONCLUSION

This article's motive is to give a brief idea about the basic implementation of multithreading on Node.js. Multithreading in Node.js is a little bit different from traditional multithreading. It is advised that for massive I/O operation main thread could do much better than worker threads. To understand more about multithreading, refer to the Node.js official document.

13

HOW TO DO STOCK TRADING WITH JAVASCRIPT

INTRODUCTION

This article's motive is to give you the vital information for building an algorithmic trading bot with Node.js, and don't take that information as financial advice. When I did little research on algorithm trading, I found out that it is costly, and only a few brokerages provide these features with high commission. Algorithm trading has incredible benefits like we don't require to waste our time by analyzing the stock price every day. It could automate our manual analysis with many stocks, so I decided to build a prototype with a simple strategy in a scalable manner.

ARCHITECTURE

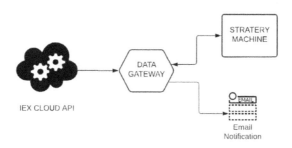

Architecture is pretty simple; it has three modules.

- Data Gateway

- Strategy Machine

- Email Notification

Data Gateway fetches the stock information from IEX Cloud API. The retrieved stock information sent to the Strategy Machine, and at their do some calculation and based on its results, select some stocks to buy. Strategy Machine will return those selected stocks to the Data Gateway. Finally, the selected stock will email us through the Email Notification Module.

Before explaining each module, it is better to explain the example strategy we are going to execute. Thus you will get an idea of how the system works and could customize strategy as you prefer.

STRATEGY

"You make your money when you buy, not when you sell."

The above quote inspires me to design the strategy we use here as an example. Once again, I remained this article is not for financial advice. The strategy is like each day; we get a company's stock prices for the last 30 days and check whether the current price is lower than the previous 30 days price. If the current price is lower than the last 30 days, we go for a buy.

DATA GATEWAY

It's an interface module that communicates with the rest of the module. Initially, Data Gateway fetches stock information from IEX Cloud API. You could also create an account at IEX Cloud and get a token for accessing the API. The collected stock information will transfer to the Strategy Machine. The Strategy Machine executes the strategy explained above, chooses some stocks based on the process, and returns them to the Data Gateway. Then Email Notification collects the selected stocks from Data Gateway and sends us through email. Data Gateway will have a setInterval function because we need to execute this strategy each day automatically.

```
const fetch = require("node-fetch");
const express = require("express");
const { strategyGenerator } =
require("./StrategyMachine");
const { emailNotification } =
require("./EmailNotification");

const app = express();
const port = 3000;
const token = "YOUR TOKEN HERE";
const getStockData = async () => {
  fetch(
```

```
`https://cloud.iexapis.com/stable/stock/mark
atch?symbols=aapl,fb&types=chart&range=1m
=30&token=${token}`
  )
    .then(async (res) => res.json())
    .then(async (stockData) => {
      const selectedStocks = await
strategyGenerator(stockData);
      await emailNotification(selectedStocks);
    });
};
const dayInMillseconds = 86400 * 1000;
setInterval(getStockData, dayInMillseconds);

app.listen(port, () => {
  console.log(`Algorithm Trading App listening
http://localhost:${port}`);
});
```

The above code snippet describes the Data
Gateway, and on line number 8, you can put
your token from IEX Cloud API. The setInterval
function on line 21 repeatedly calls the function
getStockData() each day, which performs the
task of getting data from API, sending data to
the Strategy Machine, and emailing the
selected stocks.

STRATEGY MACHINE

The Strategy Machine does the calculation for selecting the preferred stocks to buy. In our strategy, this module needs to analyze the company's stock price for 30 days. If the current price is lesser than the previous days' price, Strategy Machine adds that stock to the buy list. Refer to the below code for knowing how its works.

```
exports.strategyGenerator = async (stockInfo) =
  const selectedStocks = [];
  for (let stock in stockInfo) {
    const stockDetails = stockInfo[stock];
    const chart = stockDetails.chart;
    const stockPriceArray = [];
    for (let item of chart) {
      stockPriceArray.push(item.close);
    }
    const lowestPrice = Math.min(...stockPriceAr
    const todayChart = chart[0];
    const todayPrice = todayChart.close;
    console.log(stock," Today price :",todayPrice,"
lowest price :",lowestPrice);
    if (todayPrice === lowestPrice) {
      selectedStocks.push(stock);
    }
  }
  return selectedStocks;
};
```

The Strategy Machine is an independent module suppose to do only the calculation for selecting a preferred stock. In this module, you could define your preferred strategy and return the chosen stocks as an array to the Data Gateway.

EMAIL NOTIFICATION

Duty of Email Notification is straightforward email us the stock returns from the Strategy Machine. Email Notification code snippet is attached below.

```
const nodemailer = require("nodemailer");

const transporter = nodemailer.createTranspor
  service: "gmail",
  auth: {
   user: "youremail@gmail.com",
   pass: "yourpassword",
  },
});

const mailOptions = {
  from: "youremail@gmail.com",
  to: "myfriend@yahoo.com",
  subject: "Stocks to buy for tomorrow",
  text: "That was easy!",
};
```

```
exports.emailNotification = async (stockInfo) =>
  if (stockInfo.length > 0) {
    const message = stockInfo.join(",");
    mailOptions.text = message;
  } else {
    mailOptions.text = "Tomorrow no stocks to bu
  }
  transporter.sendMail(mailOptions, function (e
info) {
    if (error) {
      console.log(error);
    } else {
      console.log("Email sent: " + info.response);
    }
  });
```

For auth information, provide your email credentials and customize the object mailOptions on line number 11 as your preferences. If you are going to use a Gmail service like the above reference code, don't forget to enable less secure apps to access Gmail; otherwise, it will block your server's email.

CONCLUSION

I build this system only for educational purpose so don't take it as financial advice and lose your investments, even the example strategy I have described never even backtracked myself. If you have an excellent strategy, implement it in this system and backtrack with previous data. Like other algorithmic trading bots, our system won't take trades itself; it only sends you the selected stocks to buy through email. The final decision is up to you whether needed to purchase the stock or not. The system aims to provide an extra eye to watch the market.

23

HOW TO CREATE ART WITH JAVASCRIPT

INTRODUCTION

The JavaScript library p5.js enables coders to make fantastic arts by only coding. The motive of this article is to provide essential information to create art using p5.js. The library allows us to make simple kid's art to a range of highly elaborate art. The topics I am going to cover in this article are the following.

- Setting p5.js in the local environment

- Drawing an ellipse

- My creative coding art portfolio

- Resources for making intricate art

- Benefits of making art by coding

SETTING P5.JS IN THE LOCAL ENVIRONMENT

Initially, create a folder and name it as your wish; inside the folder, create two files, index.html, and sketch.js, copy the below code snippet and paste inside index.html.

```
<html>
  <head>
  <script src="https://cdn.jsdelivr.net/npm/
        p5@1.2.0/lib/p5.js">
  </script>
  <script src="sketch.js"> </script>
  </head>
  <body>
    <main>
    </main>
  </body>
</html>
```

The index.html is the entry point of our program where we load all the functions to create art using p5.js. Locally made JavaScript file sketch.js also needed to pack. The code attached below is required to place inside sketch.js.

```
function setup() {
 createCanvas(400, 400);
}
function draw() {
 background(120);
}
```

We create the canvas on the method setup() because it runs only once the program gets loaded the first time. The method draw() keeps running till the program ends, and there we define the code wanted to render on the screen. Thus we set up a p5.js environment locally. By double-clicking on index.html could see your canvas with grey color in the background.

DRAWING AN ELLIPSE

In this article, I picked draw an ellipse as a section to provide a basic idea of making shapes with code. By understanding the formula for creating an ellipse, you could make other shapes. The syntax of making an ellipse is following.

```
ellipse(x, y, w, [h])
```

x: denote the x-coordinate of the ellipse
y: denote the x-coordinate of the ellipse
w: indicate the width of the ellipse
h: indicate the height of the ellipse

MY CREATIVE CODING ART PORTFOLIO

I am not an artist; I could still create that art inside the frames with p5.js. For making such arts, you suppose to learn some math, randomness, Perlin noise, etc. It took around one month for me to understand the formula. I also make the cover picture of this article with another interesting method called generative art, where the algorithm we write automatically generates some random arts by itself.

Still, I am also a beginner in this domain; my knowledge is not enough to teach you how to make those intricate art. With only partial knowledge, it is impossible to convey things, so I decided to share all resources I used to learn.

RESOURCES FOR MAKING INTRICATE ART

My first reference is a YouTube channel named The Coding Train; where, a cool guy effortlessly teaches p5.js from basics to all the advanced topics I mentioned, like randomness, Perlin noise, etc.

After watching all his playlists go to the p5.js reference page, you get all the syntax for available functions on p5.js to start your art.

BENEFITS OF MAKING ART BY CODING

If you are not an artist and still love to make art, then creative coding with p5.js is a better option. Making art could take as a hobby and make some passive income by selling out art. Websites like Teespring and Redbubble allow us to sell wall art. We need to upload our designs to those sites, and we will get a royalty payment for each sale.

Making art with p5.js will increase your problem-solving skill because the color transformation and arranging the shapes are made of mathematical equations. Moreover, your productivity and creativity will expand.

30

HOW TO DO NLP WITH JAVASCRIPT

INTRODUCTION

It's possible to implement Natural Language Processing in your JavaScript project without integrating external API by using Cereberum.js.

Cereberum.js is an OpenSource npm package designed to perform advanced Machine Learning operations like Natural Language Processing into your JavaScript project. Mainly NLP is used for making chatbots in the web application. If the web application builds on JavaScript, it would be required to use an external API to implement a chatbot. These API might be costly; we are transferring our data to an external server for processing it could violate the privacy policy. Cerberum.js allows us to process data in your JavaScript project itself, and Cereberum.js makes the NLP implementation as easy as possible.

BASIC USAGE OF CEREBRUM.JS

To implement Cerebrum.js into your project is very easy and could be done in five steps.

- Installation: Install the Cerebrum.js package into your project by using the following command.

npm i cerebrum.js

- Importing the package: For using the Cerebrum.js built-in functions, you are supposed to import the package on which file you presume to use NLP regarding operations and create an instance. Below code, snippet shows how to import.

```
const Cerebrum = require("cerebrum.js");
const newCerebrum = new Cerebrum();
```

- Creating the dataset: This is a critical step for NLP implementation because it should be accurate; otherwise, you won't get the preferred result. Cerebrum.js take an array of objects as the dataset for training and making the model out of it. The array's length must be greater than three more each object in the array has the following property intent, utterances, and answers. Each property usage is as follows.

- intent: In the process of making the dataset, the intent is used for similar grouping kind of questions, for example, "How are you?","How do you feel?" and "Are you fine?" these questions categorized into a single intent. As intent property value, we have to provide a name like if the set of questions is asked towards a customer by the merchant, we could name it as "client.howareyou".

- utterances: It's an array of strings which include all the question in that particular intent more the question we provide more the accurate model will be for that specific context.

- answers: It is also an array of strings that include all the answers for that particular intent. When a user asks a similar kind of question, Cereberum.js will pick each answer from the array and respond. More the answers provided will avoid repetition of the same answer for the same context of questions.Below is a code snippet of the sample dataset required by the Cerebrum.js

```
const dataset = [
  {
    intent: "agent.creator",
    utterances: ["who build me", "who create
                me"],
    answers: [
      "You build me",
      "Its You",
      "You created me"
    ]
  },
  {
    intent: "agent.sing",
    utterances: [
      "do you sing song",
      "will you sing song"
    ],
    answers: [
      "Yes I do",
      "Yes I will"
    ],
  },
];
```

- Training the dataset: After creating the dataset next step is to make a model out of it; for that, we have to train the dataset. Cerebrum.js is having a function called trainCerebrum() to train the prepared dataset, and we pass the dataset as an argument to the trainCerebrum(dataSet) function for making the model. This function is asynchronous and will return the string "Success" if completed training successfully. Below is a code snippet of how to train your dataset using trainCerebrum().

```
const train = async () => {
  const response = await
  newCerebrum.trainCerebrum(dataset);
  return response;
};
```

- Getting a response from the model: If the training were successful, a file named model.nlp would be created in your root file. Using a function cerebrumReplay(), we could get the response to our question.

cerebrumReplay() takes a string as an argument could pass our question to ask into the function, and the function will return the appropriate answer for that question from the trained model. Below is a code snippet of how to get a response from the model.

```
const response = async (question) => {
  const answer = await
  newCerebrum.cerebrumReplay(question);
  return answer;
};
```

CEREBRUM.JS IMPLEMENTATION DEMO CODE

All the above step merged into a single code snippet to understand the basic working of cereberum.js

```javascript
const Cerebrum = require("cerebrum.js");

const newCerebrum = new Cerebrum();

// Dataset for training
const dataset = [
  {
    intent: "agent.creator",
    utterances: ["who build me", "who create
                me"],
    answers: [
      "You build me",
      "Its You",
      "You created me"
    ]
  },
  {
    intent: "agent.sing",
    utterances: [
      "do you sing song",
      "will you sing song"
    ],
```

```
    answers: [
      "Yes I do",
      "Yes I will"
    ],
  },
];

// Calling the training function for training
the dataset
const train = async () => {
  const response = await
  newCerebrum.trainCerebrum(dataset);
  return response;
};

train().then((v) => {
  if (v) {
    console.log(v);
  }
});

// Getting the response from trained model
const response = async (question) => {
  const answer = await
  newCerebrum.cerebrumReplay(question);
  return answer;
};
```

```
setTimeout(function () {
  response("who build me").then((v) => {
    if (v) {
      console.log(v);
    }
  });
}, 3000);

setTimeout(function () {
  response("who build me").then((v) => {
    if (v) {
      console.log(v);
    }
  });
}, 6000);
```

In the above code snippet, the package imported to the sampleCerebrumCode.js created an instance and then saved it to a constant newCerebrum. Then, another constant dataset will store the prepared dataset required to train, then a function named train() is created to call the asynchronous function trainCerebrum() provided by the Cerebrum.js. While calling the train() function, the model gets created. Another function response() to fetch the trained answers from the modal. In that function, we call the asynchronous function cerebrumReplay() and get the answer.

The above code snippet train() function once only called because the modal gets saved in the created instance newCerebrum and could use that for getting further response no need to train each time to get an answer.

BASIC ARICHETUCHRE OF THE PACKAGE

41

THE END

www.ingramcontent.com/pod-product-compliance
Lightning Source LLC
LaVergne TN
LVHW051634050326
832903LV00033B/4756